DISCOVER
The Backroads of New England

DISCOVER
The Backroads of New England

BY LOUISE QUAYLE

PHOTOGRAPHY BY

KEN ROSS & JOE VIESTI

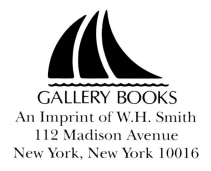

GALLERY BOOKS
An Imprint of W.H. Smith
112 Madison Avenue
New York, New York 10016

A FRIEDMAN GROUP BOOK

Published by GALLERY BOOKS
An Imprint of W. H. Smith Publishers, Inc.
112 Madison Avenue
New York, New York 10016

ISBN 0-8317-0671-6

DISCOVER THE BACKROADS OF NEW ENGLAND
was prepared and produced by
Michael Friedman Publishing Group, Inc.
15 West 26th Street
New York, New York 10010

Editor: James K. Blum
Art Director: Robert W. Kosturko
Photo Editor: Christopher C. Bain
Designer: David B. Weisman
Production Manager: Karen L. Greenberg

All photographs © Viesti Associates.
Viesti Associates is a stock-photography library
with offices in New York City and Austin, Texas.

Color separations by South Sea International Press, Ltd.
Printed and bound in Hong Kong by Leefung-Asco Printers, Ltd.

Photographs © Ken Ross 1989: 6-7, 16-17, 18, 19, 24, 26, 36, 43, 50(all), 52, 62

Photographs © Joe Viesti 1989: 3, 5, 10, 11, 12, 14-15, 17, 20-21, 22, 23, 25,
27(all), 28, 29(all), 30-31, 31, 32, 34, 37, 38, 39, 40, 41, 42, 44, 45(all), 46, 47, 48,
49, 51, 53, 54-55, 56, 57, 58, 60(all), 63, 64, 65(all), 66, 67, 68, 69, 70, 70-71, 72

C O N T E N T S

Introduction

New England is the cradle of American life–its values, its history, its pioneering spirit. For those wishing to escape religious persecution, here was a new Eden–here began the seemingly boundless frontiers of vast forests, rich soil, religious freedom, and the foundation for American democracy. The Yankee ethos played a crucial role in the founding of the new nation; it still pervades American life, literature, and politics. While the frontier quickly moved west, Yankee pluck and a stalwart determination to live the good, free life remained a mainstay of the region.

Much of New England grew around a strong sense of community. The meetinghouses, Congregational churches, and town commons throughout the region bespeak the early settlers' extensive involvement in village life. Whether used as gathering centers to make community decisions about business and farming or just to socialize, these meeting places were and are central to the lives of New England villagers. Though New Englanders have a reputation for keeping to themselves, the geography of their villages helps maintain the essence of community, and village greens still dot the New England landscape. Visitors wandering the backroads of New England may be pleasantly surprised to find many smiling, friendly faces in people known for their reserved nature.

While New England overflows with old Yankee fishing villages and town commons nestled among rolling foothills, it also boasts a rich literary and intellectual history. Nathaniel Hawthorne, Henry Wadsworth Longfellow, and Henry David Thoreau are but a few of the presences one may sense along the narrow roads and covered bridges of the heart of New England. So, too, does one sense the foundations of American democracy when passing through the region that has given the United States more politicians and statesmen than any other.

Travelers in New England enjoy some of the world's finest bed-and-breakfasts against the backdrop of the hilly landscape, and can take time to pull over for a chat with a farmer at his roadside stand or to explore a weatherworn barn chock-full of antiques. Come discover the backroads of New England and savor some of its colorful bounty.

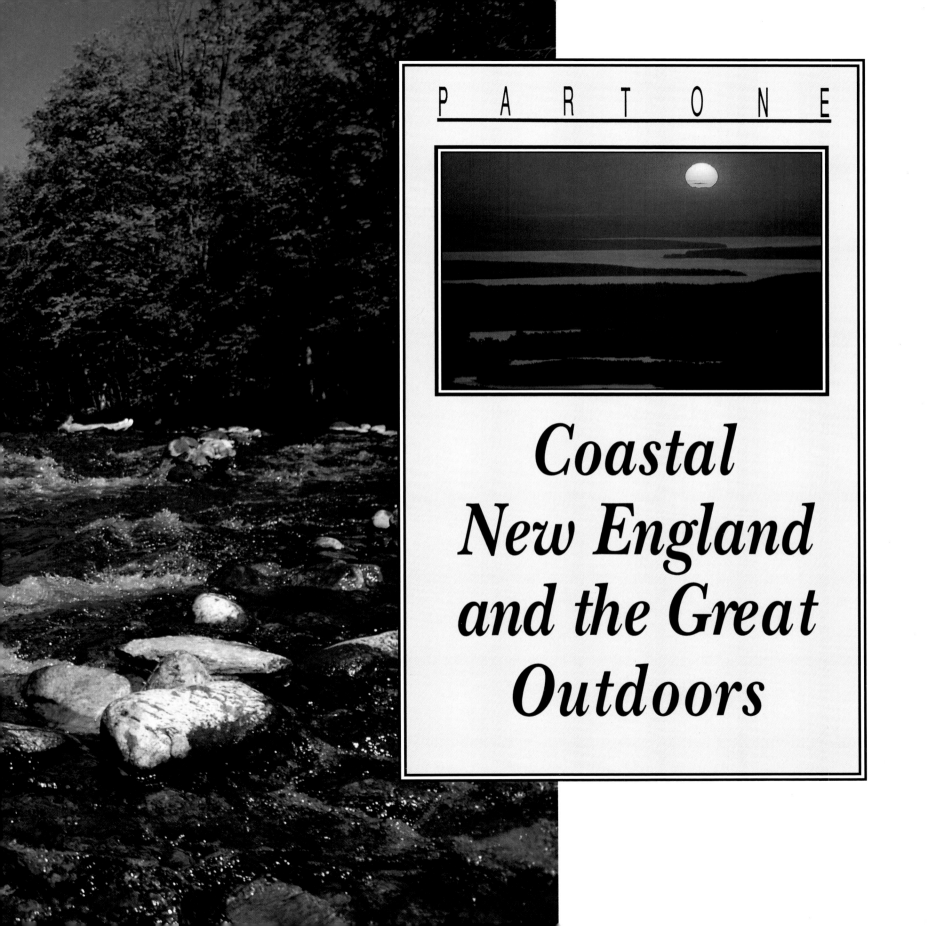

PART ONE

Coastal New England and the Great Outdoors

M any of Massachusetts's rivers (previous page) contain rapids excellent for both white-water canoeing and the less taxing sport of tubing.

Nestled in quiet, safe harbors and along craggy shores, New England fishing villages offer a picturesque view of the hard-working fisherman's life from yesterday and today. Many towns still thrive on the bounty of the sea–particularly the famous Maine lobster–yet the heyday of New England fishery has gone. Its legacy is perpetuated for visitors in the many coastal villages throughout the region.

Maine claims the first sea battle in the New World, which occurred at Machias during the Revolutionary War in 1775. The New England coast was to play a large role in many subsequent military actions. For example, though the states of New England opposed the War of 1812 (which, ironically, was fought to protect United States shipping interests), their privateering maritime adventurers amassed enormous profits, pulling in some 49 million dollars. Today mostly pleasure craft and fishing boats ply the waters of the New England coast, offering visitors

The first national park established east of the Mississippi, Maine's Acadia National Park is one of the most popular. Acadia is home to Mt. Desert Island's amazing 32 thousand acres. The 120 miles of trails, 57 miles of carriage paths (built by John D. Rockefeller, Jr.), and 26-mile loop road around the island's circumference offer unlimited wilderness experiences as well as breathtaking scenery.

*P*leasure boats fill the harbors of many quiet coastal villages. Rockport, Maine, famous for its rocky coastline, is no exception.

access to coastal Maine's numerous seaside parks, alluring islands, and wondrous views of its rugged shores.

Ship building also thrived in New England among the rich forests of Vermont, New Hampshire, and Maine. The New England ship-building industry had its roots in the Popham Colony, settled in 1607 where Phippsburg, Maine is today. The profitable whaling and sea-trading industries that grew there gave rise to busy ship-building ports like the one in Bath, Maine.

Although the sea dominates the imaginations of many when they think of New England, inland settlers of this corner of the United States enjoy equally breathtaking scenery. Inland mountains, rich forests, rapid rivers, and tranquil lakes offered abundant crops to its first settlers and unsurpassed recreation to the post-agricultural society of the late-nineteenth and twentieth centuries. Sports enthusiasts flock to New England for fishing, canoeing, and swimming–and colorful balloons may even decorate the sky here and there.

*R*ecalling Maine's first inhabitants, the Native American tribes, a canoe glides silently through the early morning fog on a Maine lake.

*S*norkeling in one of the many area lakes is a cool summer activity in Rockport, Maine.

*L*ighthouses, the beacons that once warned ships of the rocky New England coasts, are mostly museum pieces now. But this lighthouse, the Quoddy Head Lighthouse in Quoddyhead, Maine, still lights the way for sailors after dark.

*M*artha's Vineyard, a tiny
island off the coast of Cape Cod,
attracts thousands of tourists--and
boats--each year.

Wilderness areas in Vermont offer fly-fishermen quiet solitude–until a deer interrupts their sport.

*V*ermont's intricate and extensive system of rivers and lakes has attracted fishermen for over one hundred years.   The

Battenkill River is a fly-fisherman's favorite.

*W*hite Mountains National Park dominates the northern New Hampshire landscape.   The Flume, a ravine carved

by glaciers, provides an unequalled hiking experience for nature enthusiasts.

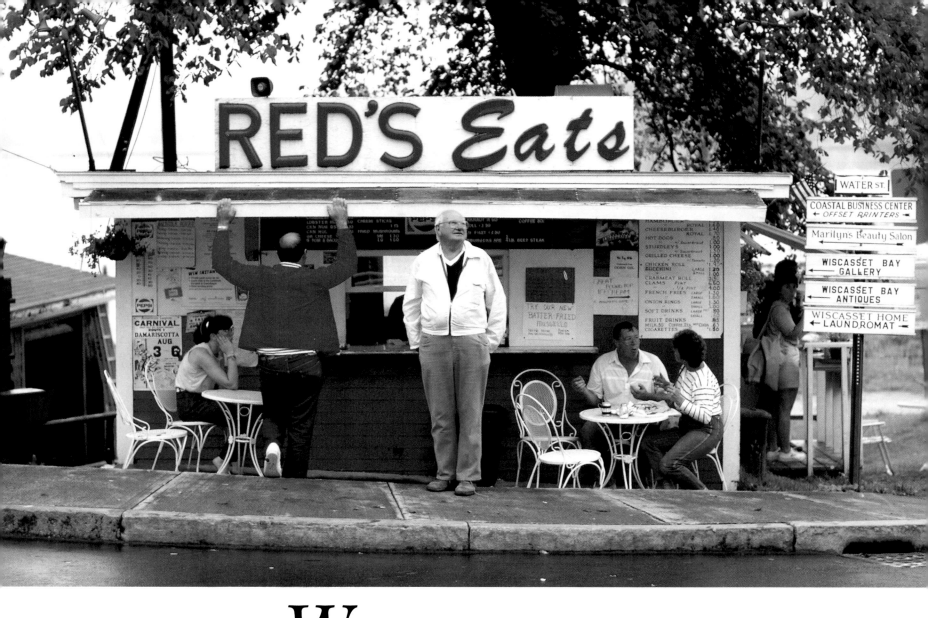

W*iscasset, Maine was a major seaport and at one time exported ships'*
masts and spars. It was once home port for an amazing thirty-five square-riggers.
Wiscasset also has its literary history–James Fenimore Cooper based Tale of the
Sea *on his experiences on the* Stirling, *which he boarded there in 1806. As with*
much of Maine, the town's economy now depends on the tourist trade.

*T*he site of the first settlement in New England, Plymouth draws thousands of tourists each year to its Pilgrim Hall Museum and Plimouth Plantation, a re-creation of life in early Plymouth. Here, the more recent trappings of its once coastal economy are displayed in old New England fashion.

*N*ewport, *Rhode Island is home to the*
International Tennis Hall of Fame. With its history of
entertaining America's elite, Newport is the perfect host
to this genteel and gracious sport.

*E*ntertainment in New England ranges from child's play on the Alpine Slide in Bromley, Vermont to the more sophisticated horse racing in Great Barrington, Massachusetts.

*H*ot-air ballooning has become a favorite pastime in the Berkshire Mountains of Massachusetts. Also known as aerostation, ballooning is more popular than ever. Each year, ballooning festivals in the region host hare-and-hound races and altitude-keeping contests. Since 1980, the number of balloons registered in the United States has more than doubled.

*G*liding, like hot-air ballooning, is a popular sport in New England. Silently riding the wind, this glider pilot enjoys one of the best available views of Vermont's mountainous landscape.

Country Inns and Backroads

*T*ree-lined roads and highways crisscross the New England landscape (previous page). Every year thousands of people enjoy the region's spectacular fall foliage.

The small New England village–from its seventeenth-century meetinghouses and cottages to its eighteenth- and nineteenth-century saltboxes and Federal-style brick buildings–remains foremost in the imaginations of many of the region's visitors. Settled around a green, or common, the New England village bespeaks a bygone era rooted in cooperative, if sometimes strict, living. At town meetings, every man had a say in governing his small community; at the Congregational Church, every man could speak his mind on religious affairs. Though the Puritans were in many ways as rigid and exclusionary as the government in England from which they escaped, the roots of religious freedom in America grew in New England.

Rhode Island, to which Roger Williams and Anne Hutchinson fled to found a truly free colony, distinguishes itself with its sprawling town layouts as well as its religious heritage. Rather than building their towns around a common, Rhode Island communities grew around large plantations; however, houses there maintain characteristics unique to New England architecture. The milder climate led to the construction of "stone ender"

Weather vanes depicting everything from fish to pheasants to pigs dot the tops of homes and barns across the New England countryside. In Great Barrington, Massachusetts, visitors can choose from a wide variety of these precious collectibles.

*T*he county courthouse has tra-
ditonally been a central part of small-
town New England life. In
Newfane, Vermont the Windham
County Courthouse illustrates an
architectural blend of the classic
Federal style with Greek revival
columns and cornices.

one- or two- room homes. Many New Hampshire and Vermont villages built along rivers or in valleys also lacked a common, but throughout New England the meetinghouse served an important function as the town center.

Until this century, travel across the hilly and forested terrain of the region was difficult. Before the Revolution, roads were rutted and muddy; land travel was slow, at best. To join the new states into a unified country, individual investors created a system of toll roads–turnpikes–that led cost-conscious travelers to "shunpike." The shunpikes, short roundabout roads for avoiding tolls, and the turnpikes laid the groundwork for the scenic roads and byways so famous today.

Today's New England is dotted with homes converted into luxurious and countrified inns that welcome travelers with old-style New England hospitality. Traveling the region's backroads, visitors will find antiques, old farmsteads, and country crafts as well as more modern telephone wires and satellite dishes. But no matter where the road takes them, wanderers through New England will always find friendly, helpful people, a delicious meal, and a comfortable bed after a long day's journey.

*B*rick buildings like this one in Salem echo the Federal-style building boom that took place in the forty years following the Revolution. Examples of the work of the city's most famous architect, Samuel McIntyre, abound in the area. Charles Bulfinch, basing his designs on those of the Englishman Robert Adam, is credited with introducing the Federal style to the New World. McIntyre in turn drew much of his inspiration from the buildings designed by Bulfinch.

*I*n Norwich, Vermont the ubiquitous white-steepled New England town buildings play host to a game relatively new to America–soccer.

*N*ewfane, Vermont's Newfane Inn offers guests comfortable accommodations as well as manicured grounds for a relaxing stroll after dinner. Here, the chef takes time out from serving his tasty fare to fatten up the trout in the stream that runs through the grounds.

*W*ith its fan and sidelights, the entrance to the Crabapple Inn in West Plymouth, New Hampshire (opposite page) is a classic example of Federal design. Federal-style buildings have four tall windows on the first floor, five on the second (often with a Palladian window in the center), and five smaller windows on the top floor that echo the style of the first two floors.

*I*n a clapboard variation on the Federal theme, Littleton, New Hampshire's Beal House Country Inn (above and right) carries the country motif inside with Americana furnishings, colorful rag rugs, and decorative tableware.

*F*or antique lovers, New England offers a collector's haven. What better place to browse for old farm implements or country furnishings than in the Eden Notch Barn in Vermont?

*N*ew England's backroads are not without surprises. A satellite dish beside a small house in Bridgewater, Maine reflects the contemporary interests of its inhabitants.

43

*O*n the front porch of the Red Lion Inn in Stockbridge, Massachusetts, visitors take a few moments to read and relax, much as Henry Wadsworth Longfellow may have done when he stayed here during the mid-1800s while courting his bride-to-be, Fanny Appleton. It was in Stockbridge that the Berkshire Congress met in 1774 to decide how they would protect their rights against the British Crown; during the 1960s, Arlo Guthrie wrote a well-known song dealing with similar questions based on his experiences here at Alice's Restaurant.

*C*ountry crafts have become a national craze–and New England offers some of the best. In Groton, Vermont, Country Lane offers handmade items from yard ornaments to hand-stitched pillows.

A slightly more sophisticated approach to antique dealing is offered by The Marston House American Antiques, which offers bed-and-breakfast accommodations to supplement its income–and perhaps entice buyers.

45

*S*teeped in Revolutionary spirit, the Griswold Inn in Essex, Connecticut flies the bicentennial flag. Visitors may feel as though they are stepping back in time when they pull up to the curb behind a horse-drawn carriage.

*T*he literary and artistic talents of many New England residents have gained worldwide renown. David Chester French, the sculptor of the Lincoln Memorial, lived in Chesterwood, Massachusetts, where he created this model of the famous memorial in his studio.

*T*he Revolutionary War battle at Concord, Massachusetts was the stage for "the shot heard 'round the world." The British troops first marched through Lexington's town common, now called Battle Green, where 130 American soldiers had assembled. After a skirmish that lasted only a few minutes–leaving eight Minutemen dead–the British marched on to Concord. In this reenactment of the scene, the Minutemen march across North Bridge, sending the British into a retreat to Boston and winning the first battle of the Revolutionary War.

*M*odern New England cottages offer old New England atmosphere. Here a man enjoys the crisp fall air under his colorful maple tree.

*W*hile traveling the backroads of New England, collectors will often find such modern items for sale as this collection of distinctive hubcaps in Bridgewater, Maine.

*M*odern additions to the village common include elaborate or simple fountains, manicured gardens, and latticed gazebos. During Revolutionary days, the common was a place to gather–here the "Minutemen" would muster in preparation for battle with the British forces. In more peaceful times, the village green is a perfect place for study or quiet contemplation.

*T*hough Shaker implements and furniture are now prized museum pieces and collectors' items, the Shaker way of life lives on at Maine's Sabbath Day Lake, at Canterbury, New Hampshire, and at the restored Shaker Village in Hancock, Massachusetts. Founded by Ann Lee, the Shaker sect lives by the saying, "Put your hands to work and your hearts to God." Indeed, as Christina Tree points out, Shakers "turned farming, craftsmanship and invention into visible prayers." One Shaker woman does just that by weaving beautiful and functional rag rugs.

*T*his massive church on Route 1 in North London, Maine reflects the French-Catholic influence that pervades the region. Note the stained-glass windows and unusual towers.

*C*overed bridges were developed by Yankee road builders to protect the structures from rotting as a result of the constant onslaught of wet New England weather. Once a common sight along Vermont roads, two hundred covered bridges were destroyed in a single year, 1927. One hundred twelve still span Vermont's waterways and New Hampshire can boast fifty-eight, while Massachusetts counts only ten covered bridges still in existence.

Bounty of the Harvest

*O*nce necessary to keep birds and other pests away from cornfields, scarecrows today are something of an art form (previous page). This family, dressed in their Sunday best, happily poses outside their home.

Nothing brings New England to mind more than the reds, golds, and yellows of autumn. Each year, foliage tours and harvest festivals celebrate the myriad hues of this region's special season. Young and old alike anticipate the coming holiday feasts, the fun of picking pumpkins fresh from the patch, and the simple enjoyment of the offerings of the land.

Farming in New England has been difficult since Massasoit and Samoset first taught the Pilgrims to cultivate the North American soil. Farmers often spent months or even years clearing the rocky soil, and until the Revolution practiced little in the way of crop rotation to maximize the land's output. After the Revolution, many farmers were in debt and at risk of losing their land. One such man, Daniel Shays of Pelham, Massachusetts, fled with 150 of his neighbors to what is now Vermont to start fresh and establish a new state. The Green Mountain State accepted produce as legal tender and was, on the whole, very hospitable to farmers.

East Burke, Vermont is one of the many communities in New England that hosts a fall foliage celebration. The fair offers farmers an opportunity to sell their produce and provides an outlet for local craftspeople as well. Here, a table full of manufactured and handmade Christmas decorations heralds the chill of winter as well as the warmth of the holiday season.

*D*ried Indian corn, herbs, and fragrant sachets of potpourri set the color scheme for fall festivals.

Water-powered stone gristmills like this one were the first mills to be built in New England. These mills ground corn and wheat to produce cornmeal and flour. Between the seventeenth and nineteenth centuries, most New England villages had three types of mills: gristmills, sawmills, and fulling mills, which cleaned, felted, and shrank dirty wool as it came off the loom.

Agriculture was not to remain a main source of income for New England states for long, however. With overcrowding and routes opening to the rich lands of the Midwest during the nineteenth century, New England farmers faced yet another struggle to remain viable. In response, they formed agricultural organizations in a final attempt to salvage their dwindling prospects. Their efforts have paid off, and the agricultural economy in New England today, though altered, thrives.

The same rejuvenating spirit pervades the agricultural and foliage fairs held in the region. From the tobacco fields of Connecticut to the more recently settled farmlands of Vermont, New Englanders and their guests revel in the spirit of the old-fashioned autumn harvest.

*W*hen settlers first arrived in the New World, they found mostly hilly, tree-covered terrain. Yet New England has its share of flat land as well, such as this farm on Route 1 in Van Buren, Maine.

*W*hat could be more fall-like than a trip to the pumpkin patch? Three harvesters display East Burke's bountiful pickings.

*C*olors–and colorful smiles– are the rule during Groton, Vermont's annual fall fair.

*T*he fall festival in Groton, Vermont brings out the old and the not-so-old to celebrate bygone eras with the year's new crop. A vintage fire engine and an antique automobile represent a part of Vermont's heritage.

*E*ven the Cub Scouts, on a break from other festival activities, take some time to be just plain silly—which is exactly what town fairs call for.

*I*n autumn harvest festivals across New England, residents enjoy the best of the new year's crop. Here, children demonstrate a waterless way to bob for apples.

*C*onnecticut's rich soil has been home to tobacco fields for hundreds of years.

*S*ince 1762, the Bradley Farm, located in the Berkshire Mountains of Massachusetts, has reaped an annual harvest. With tourism at a peak in the area, the farm now offers homemade cornhusk dolls and brooms, dried flower arrangements, and other fall decorations along with its harvest of squash, tomatoes, and more.

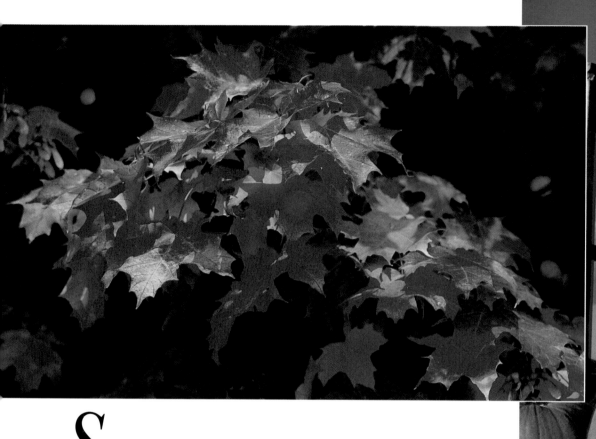

*S*ure to turn heads with their beautiful colors, Vermont's maple trees also excite the tastebuds with the delicious syrups and candies they provide.

*D*uring the summer and fall, roadside stands throughout New England offer passersby the freshest and finest produce available. Few could fail to be impressed with these pumpkins.

*T*he White River Farm in Vermont is nearly overcome by pumpkins during the harvest season. Patches such as this one are common throughout New England.